SOCIAL
MEDIA
SENSATIONS

# Twitter

## Joanne Mattern

**Checkerboard Library**

An Imprint of Abdo Publishing
abdopublishing.com

# abdopublishing.com

Published by Abdo Publishing, a division of ABDO, PO Box 398166, Minneapolis, Minnesota 55439. Copyright © 2017 by Abdo Consulting Group, Inc. International copyrights reserved in all countries. No part of this book may be reproduced in any form without written permission from the publisher. Checkerboard Library™ is a trademark and logo of Abdo Publishing.

Printed in the United States of America, North Mankato, Minnesota
062016
092016

THIS BOOK CONTAINS RECYCLED MATERIALS

Design: Emily Love, Mighty Media, Inc.
Production: Mighty Media, Inc.
Editor: Liz Salzmann
Cover Photos: Shutterstock
Interior Photos: AP Images, pp. 11, 19; Getty Images, pp. 9, 15, 21, 23; iStockphoto, pp. 5, 25; Jack Dorsey, p. 13; Shutterstock, pp. 4, 5, 6, 7, 17, 18, 27, 29

**Publishers Cataloging-in-Publication Data**
Names: Mattern, Joanne, author.
Title: Twitter / by Joanne Mattern.
Description: Minneapolis, MN : Abdo Publishing, [2017] | Series: Social media sensations | Includes index.
Identifiers: LCCN 2016934277 | ISBN 9781680781939 (lib. bdg.) | ISBN 9781680775785 (ebook)
Subjects: LCSH: Twitter (Firm)--Juvenile literature. | Twitter--Juvenile literature. | Online social networks--United States--Juvenile literature. | Internet industry--United States--Juvenile literature.
Classification: DDC 338.4--dc23
LC record available at /http://lccn.loc.gov/2016934277

# Contents

# Twitter

**URL:** https://www.twitter.com

**PURPOSE:** Twitter is an **online** social-**networking** service that allows users to post short messages.

**CURRENT CEO:** Jack Dorsey

**NUMBER OF USERS:**
More than 300 million

**MARCH 2006**
Twitter is launched as twttr.com

**MARCH 2007**
Twitter is featured at the South by Southwest festival, greatly increasing its popularity

**AUGUST 2007**
The hashtag appears on Twitter for the first time

**JANUARY 2013**
Twitter launches the video service Vine

# Meet the Founders

**JACK DORSEY** was born in Saint Louis, Missouri, on November 19, 1976. Dorsey attended college in Missouri and then New York. He then moved to California to work in technology.

**EVAN WILLIAMS** was born on March 31, 1972. He grew up on a farm in Nebraska. He attended the University of Nebraska in Lincoln. But Williams left college to start working. He moved to California and created a software company called Pyra Labs.

**CHRISTOPHER "BIZ" STONE** was born on March 10, 1974, in Boston, Massachusetts. He attended college in Massachusetts before leaving school to work at technology companies in California.

Evan Williams

Christopher "Biz" Stone

Jack Dorsey

# CHAPTER 1

# What Is Twitter?

**Y**ou're at a baseball game watching your favorite team win.  Suddenly, a foul ball flies toward you.  You catch it!  You want to share your excitement with all your friends.  So you quickly log on to Twitter and send out a tweet.  Instantly, your friends and followers learn about your awesome experience.  That's the magic of Twitter!

Twitter is a social-**networking** service that allows users to post messages called tweets.  Tweets are meant to be short.  They cannot be longer than 140 characters.  Many users find short messages to be less overwhelming than the long posts

*Twitter is a website and an app. Many people tweet using the app on their smartphones and tablets.*

*Twitter messages often describe how users feel or what they are doing at one exact moment.*

on other social media sites.  Users can also include photos, videos, or links with their tweets.

Twitter users see others' tweets by visiting their profiles.  They can also follow one another to receive tweets in a **feed**.  Users communicate back and forth on Twitter and share others' tweets.  In this way, a Twitter message can go **viral**.  It can be seen by thousands, or even millions, of people in seconds!

# CHAPTER 2

# How Twitter Began

**A**ccording to Twitter co-founder Jack Dorsey, the idea for Twitter was born on a playground.  In 2006, Dorsey was a **software** engineer at a company called Odeo.  One day, he was at a park with some coworkers.  They were thinking about new ideas for the company.

Dorsey was on top of a slide when he had an idea. He wanted to create a system for sending short **status updates**.  The system would easily broadcast a status update to a **network** of people using text messaging.

Dorsey shared his idea with Odeo coworkers Evan Williams and Christopher "Biz" Stone.  Together, they created an early **version** of Twitter.  This early version of the service used a fairly simple system.

Users of this new service could choose which people they wanted in their network.  Then, they could text messages to the **short code** 40404.  This would cause

*Jack Dorsey (left) and Christopher "Biz" Stone (right)
created their early version of Twitter in just two weeks.*

the system to send the messages to everyone in their
**network**.  The team got to work developing and naming
their new service.

# CHAPTER 3

# What's in a Name?

**A**s they completed development of their new service, Dorsey, Williams, and Stone began thinking of a name for it. They wanted something short and catchy. They also wanted the name to capture the feeling of a cell phone constantly vibrating with notifications from friends.

Dorsey discussed name ideas with coworkers and friends. They searched dictionaries for the right word. They came across the words *jitter* and *twitch*. But neither felt right. The team kept searching.

Then Odeo employee Noah Glass came across the word *twitter*. Its definitions were "a short burst of **inconsequential** information" and "chirps from birds." The founders liked it! Now that they had a name, launching the service was the next step.

*Evan Williams in the Odeo offices in 2006. The technology company helped people publish audio content.*

# CHAPTER 4

# Public Launch

The Twitter service was originally used only on cell phones. At the time, many phones had a limit of 160 characters for a text message. So, Twitter's founders set the limit for Twitter messages to 140 characters. This left 20 characters for the user's name to fit in with a text.

The founders also shortened the service's name from Twitter to Twttr. There were two reasons for this. The first was so the name would have five letters. This was to match the length of numbers in the **short code** to which users sent messages. The second was that the website address twitter.com was already taken.

At first, only Odeo's employees could use Twttr. And they loved it! By summer, several employees were using the service so often that their cell phone bills were enormous. Some racked up hundreds of dollars' worth of Twttr messages!

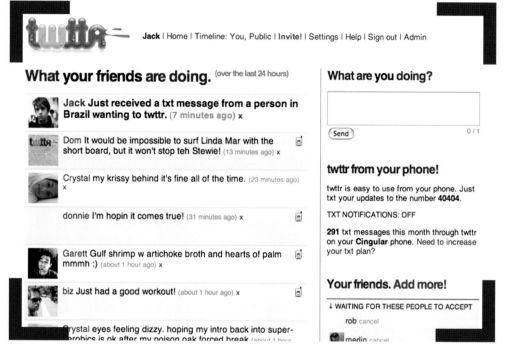

*Dorsey's Twttr page in summer 2006*

On March 21, 2006, twttr.com was launched as a public service. But it was slow to catch on with users outside of Odeo. Then, that August, Stone received a tweet about a nearby earthquake. Seconds later, he felt the quake.

The tweet had traveled faster than the quake! The founders knew Twttr was special. They kept promoting the service so the rest of the world would realize it too.

# CHAPTER 5

# Early Explosion

**W**ithin six months of launching, Twttr was beginning to slowly gain users. The founders decided to switch the service's name back to Twitter. They bought the **domain name** twitter.com. By early 2007, a few thousand tweets a day were showing up on the site.

Keeping its busy site running cost Twitter a lot of money. The founders had to pay for office space, equipment, and employee salaries. To make money, Twitter started allowing ads on the site. Companies would pay Twitter to host these ads. In return, the companies' messages would be shared with Twitter users.

However, Twitter needed to gain more users so companies would want to advertise on the service. The founders needed to do some advertising of their own. They decided a big event would help spread the word.

In March 2007, Twitter set up huge computer screens at South by Southwest (SXSW) in Austin, Texas. SXSW is a

*During the 2007 SXSW festival, Twitter usage tripled. The average number of tweets per day rose from 20,000 to 60,000.*

music, film, and **technology** festival.  Attendees could sign up for Twitter and tweet about what they were doing.

The tweets appeared on the big screens at the festival. The more tweets people saw, the more they wanted to send their own.  That SXSW is considered to be the start of Twitter's popularity.

# CHAPTER 6

# Tweeting

Since its success at SXSW, Twitter has become popular around the world.  People use Twitter to communicate with others about what they are thinking or doing.  Users can also choose to follow other users.  Then the users receive all of the tweets posted by the people they follow.

A user can also retweet a message.  When a user retweets a message, all of his or her followers can see it.  In this way, a tweet can spread quickly far beyond the poster's original followers.

Celebrities and corporations make use of Twitter as well.  Celebrities use the site to promote projects and build personal connections with their fans.  Corporations use Twitter to advertise products and services.

In 2011, Twitter allowed its users to post photos along with their tweets.  This function became very popular with users.  It also provided celebrities and companies even more ways to promote themselves and their products.

*As of 2015, singer Katy Perry had 71 million followers.*
*That was the most followers of any Twitter user.*

# CHAPTER 7

# Tags and Hashtags

**W**ith so many tweets coming and going, it can be hard for followers to read everything in their **feeds**. Tagging allows users to make sure their tweets show up in certain followers' feeds.

A tag is the @ symbol followed by the person's Twitter username. A tagged tweet will go to the person's feed even if he or she doesn't follow the sender. Twitter users can also choose to view only tweets in which they are tagged.

*There are about 20 new tweets each hour with the hashtag #funnycats.*

Twitter introduced hashtags in August 2007. Hashtags group tweets together by topic. A hashtag is the hash symbol (#) followed by a word or phrase. Twitter users can search for tweets that include the same hashtag.

For example, users could search for #funnycats to find funny tweets about cats. This shows the user all tweets with that hashtag, including tweets from people the user is not following.

## Hashtag

Hashtags make grouping Twitter content manageable. Twitter uses a search engine function to sort hashtags. Site engineers write codes so that words with the # symbol before them are searchable. The hashtag turns into a link that users can click to navigate to the topic.

There are certain rules all hashtags must follow in order to work properly. Twitter hashtags can be any combination of letters and numbers. Hashtags cannot be all numbers and cannot include any spaces.

# CHAPTER 8

# Viral Tweets

Every day, Twitter users post 500 million tweets. This number grows even higher during major events. Twitter users can follow live events without watching them. For example, fans at a football game might tweet about each play. Their followers can read these tweets to stay connected to the game without watching it.

Twitter also keeps a list of trending hashtag topics. This list shows what topics are tweeted about and then retweeted the most. This provides users an up-to-the-minute look at what's happening around the world.

## Did You Know?

The most tweeted event in history was Germany's victory over Brazil in the 2014 FIFA World Cup. According to Twitter, users sent about 35.6 million tweets during the game.

Remember that when users click on a hashtag, they see all related tweets, from users they follow and do not follow. This can cause tweets to go **viral**. They can be seen and shared by millions of users.

At the 2014 Academy Awards, someone tweeted a photo of host Ellen DeGeneres taking a **selfie** with several actors. The hashtag was #Oscars. The photo received more than 2 million retweets, setting a new record.

# CHAPTER 9

# World Events

Twitter does more than just allow people to experience entertainment and popular events. It is also a great tool for sharing news about world events. During natural **disasters**, tweeting is a simple, quick way for people to reach out to others. Disaster victims can use Twitter to report on conditions and ask for help. Relief organizations use Twitter to respond to people in need.

Twitter can also keep people informed during political **uprisings**. In 2011, Twitter users around the world read first-hand accounts of a revolution in Egypt. Twitter users there tweeted about what was going on. This helped spread the uprising. Because of this, some governments have blocked Twitter during times of political **unrest**. However, these efforts have mostly been unsuccessful.

*Thousands of Egyptians used Twitter to organize protests in 2011. Many used the hashtag #Egypt.*

# CHAPTER 10

# Effects and Safety

**T**witter can have a huge effect on its users' lives. The service makes it easy for people to share what is happening to them the instant it happens.  This can be a good thing, because it allows people to stay in touch. However, some people feel this constant communication is distracting.  Critics think continual **status updates** make little things seem very important when they really are not.

**Cyberbullying** has become a problem on Twitter. People often post comments without thinking that their words might offend someone.  A joke at someone else's expense could go **viral**.  This could make the person feel bad about himself or herself.  As with all social media, it is important to use Twitter safely.  And users should report cyberbullying to a trusted adult.

*Ninety-two percent of teens age 12 to 17 use the Internet daily, many on their smartphones and tablets.*

# CHAPTER 11

# Future of Twitter

**S**ocial media users are always looking for new ways to communicate. Twitter has had to adapt to ever-changing technology. Shortly after its addition of photos, Twitter allowed users to post videos in their tweets.

In 2012, Twitter acquired a video service called Vine. The service had become popular with a small group of users, but had not been publicly launched. Twitter launched Vine in January 2013. This allowed Vine users to post six-second videos on Twitter.

Twitter bought Periscope in 2015. It is a service that allows users to post live interactive videos. The videos are visible to all of a user's followers at once. Viewers can post comments and questions while they watch. Then, the video creator can respond through the video.

Today, Twitter has grown to more than 300 million active users. It has transformed from a texting app between coworkers to a worldwide social media platform.

*Twitter connects people, promotes businesses, and shares news.  And it does it in 140 characters or less!*

What will the Twitter of the future look like?  It may add new features.  But Twitter is likely to remain an important method for people to stay connected to each other.

A Twitter user must be at least 13 to have an account.

Users can sign up at twitter.com. Or they can download the app to their smartphones or tablets.

Once signed up, users can start tweeting!  They should make sure to use Twitter safely.  Users shouldn't reveal their full names or home addresses in their tweets.  Users shouldn't ever agree to meet a stranger who contacts them on Twitter.

Users can look for interesting people to follow.  This could include their friends and family members.  Users can also follow their favorite celebrities, athletes, or organizations.

If a user gets bullied or bothered by another user on Twitter, he or she can block that user.  Users can also report bullies and inappropriate content to Twitter.

Have fun on Twitter. Connect with friends. Follow interesting **feeds**. Express yourself. Get creative! Twitter is a great resource as long as you use it responsibly.

# Glossary

**cyberbully** – to tease, hurt, or threaten someone online.

**disaster** – an event that causes damage, destruction, and often loss of life. Natural disasters include events such as hurricanes, tornadoes, and earthquakes.

**domain name** – a name that is the general internet address for a website.

**download** – to transfer data from a computer network to a single computer or device.

**feed** – a constantly updating list of online posts.

**inappropriate** – not suitable, fitting, or proper.

**inconsequential** – small or not important.

**network** – to join or communicate with a group of people. The group is also called a network.

**online** – connected to the Internet.

**selfie** – an image of oneself taken by oneself using a digital camera, especially for posting on social networks.

**short code** – a special telephone number used to send text messages.

**software** – the written programs used to operate a computer.

**status update** – a post on social media that describes what the poster is doing or feeling.

**technology** – the science of how something works.

**unrest** – a situation in which many of the people in a country are angry and hold protests or act violently.

**uprising** – a usually local act of violence against a state, a country, or a ruler.

**version** – a different form or type of an original.

**viral** – quickly or widely spread, usually by electronic communication.

## Websites

To learn more about Social Media Sensations, visit **booklinks.abdopublishing.com**. These links are routinely monitored and updated to provide the most current information available.

# Index